THE OCEANS EXPLORED
Claudia Martin
OCEAN LIFE
Illustrated by Fiona Osbaldstone
I0759738
PowerKiDS press

Published in 2026
by The Rosen Publishing Group, Inc.
2544 Clinton Street, Buffalo, NY 14224

First published in 2021 in Great Britain by Wayland

Credits

Author and editor: Claudia Martin
Illustrator: Fiona Osbaldstone
Designer: Dan Prescott, Couper Street Type Co.
Proofreader: Annabel Savery

The publisher would like to thank the following for permission to reproduce their photographs: Alamy: WaterFrame 5tl, Alex Mustard/Nature Picture Library 10, Daniel Lamborn 16, Pascal Kobeh/Nature Picture Library 24, Steven Kovacs/BIOSPHOTO 26; Getty Images: johnandersonphoto/iStock 9, Fiona Ayerst/iStock 13, scottdart/iStock 19, Vicki Jauron, Babylon and Beyond Photography 20, Dmitry Miroshnikov 23, pilesasmiles/iStock 28; Shutterstock: Agami Photo Agency 4l, Steven Russell Smith 4r, Rich Carey 5tr, Istvan Kovacs 5b, Sergey Uryadnikov 7, Lee Yiu Tung 15.

Cataloging-in-Publication Data

Names: Martin, Claudia, author. | Osbaldstone, Fiona, illustrator.
Title: Ocean life / by Claudia Martin, illustrated by Fiona Osbaldstone.
Description: Buffalo, NY : PowerKids Press, 2026. | Series: The oceans explored | Includes glossary and index.
Identifiers: ISBN 9781499454000 (pbk.) | ISBN 9781499454017 (library bound) | ISBN 9781499454024 (ebook)
Subjects: LCSH: Marine organisms--Juvenile literature. | Marine plants--Juvenile literature. |
Marine animals--Juvenile literature.
Classification: LCC QH91.16 M378 2026 | DDC 578.77--dc23

Manufactured in the United States of America
CPSIA Compliance Information: Batch #CSPK26. For further information contact Rosen Publishing at 1-800-237-9932.

CONTENTS

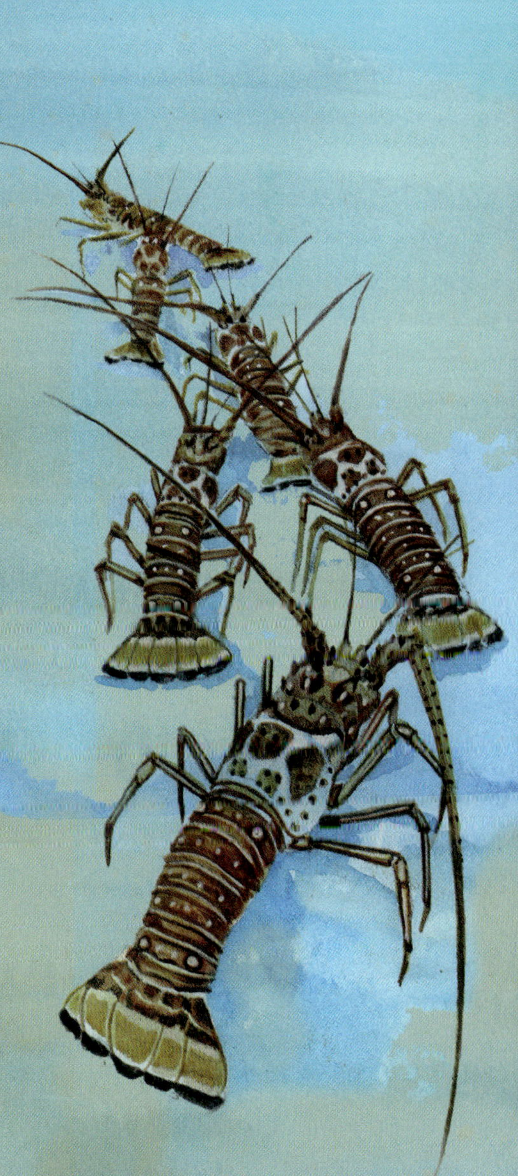

OCEAN LIFE

The oceans are home to trillions of living things, from huge whales to tiny floating plants. Five types of animals live in and around the oceans: invertebrates, fish, mammals, reptiles, and birds. These animals feed on each other, forming food webs. Some animals hunt smaller creatures, while others eat plants or seaweeds, which make their own food from sunlight.

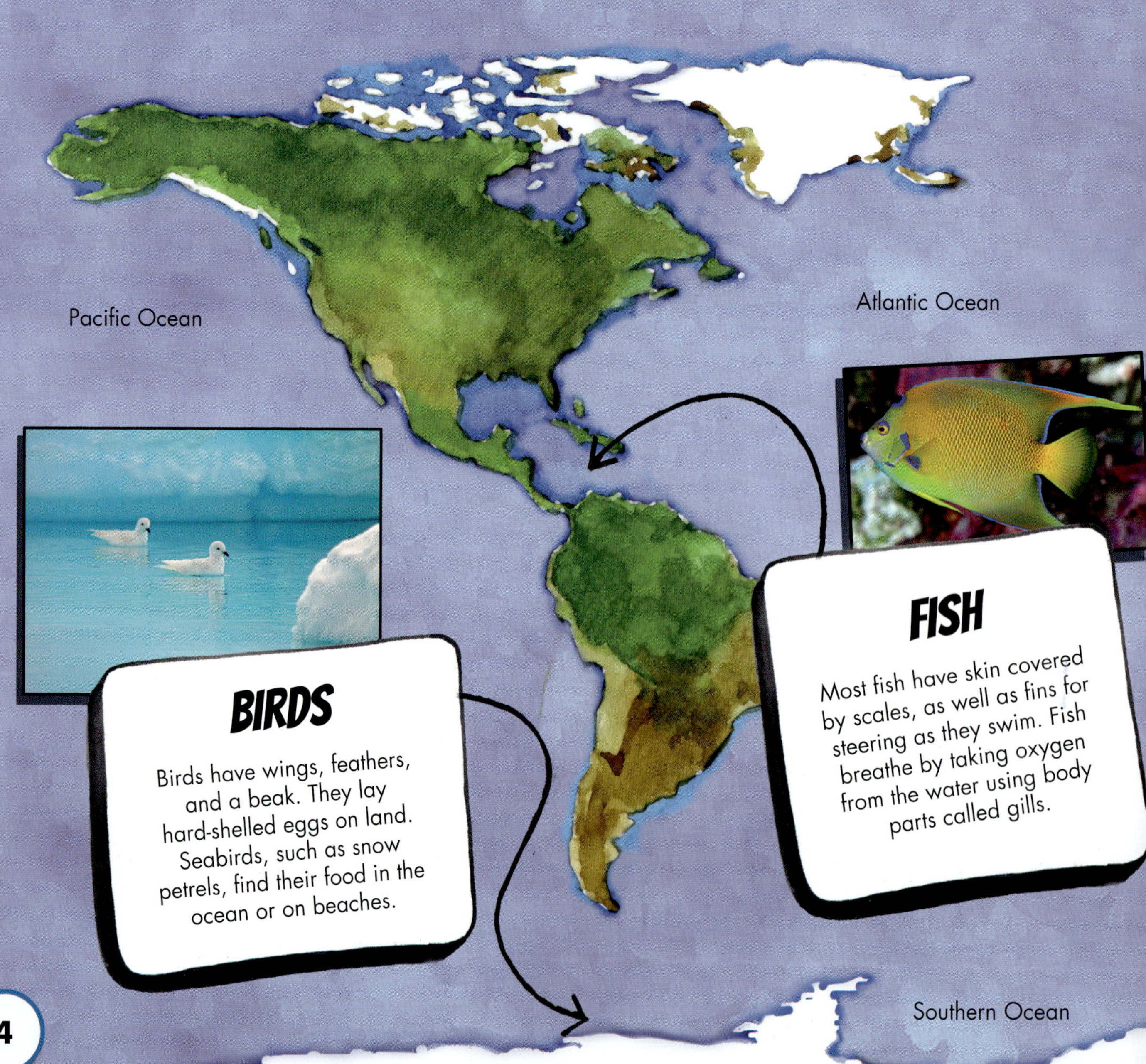

BIRDS

Birds have wings, feathers, and a beak. They lay hard-shelled eggs on land. Seabirds, such as snow petrels, find their food in the ocean or on beaches.

FISH

Most fish have skin covered by scales, as well as fins for steering as they swim. Fish breathe by taking oxygen from the water using body parts called gills.

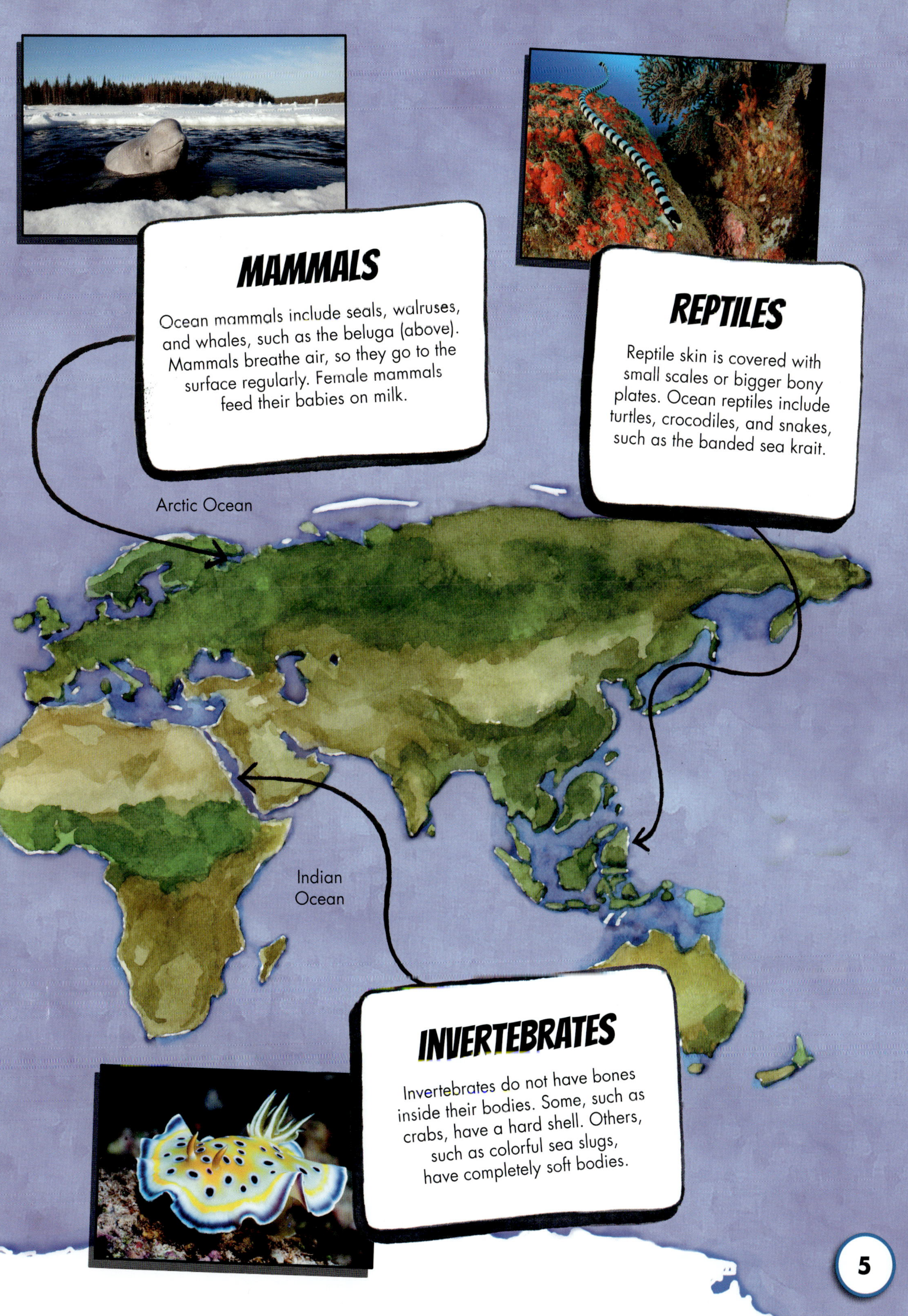

MAMMALS

Ocean mammals include seals, walruses, and whales, such as the beluga (above). Mammals breathe air, so they go to the surface regularly. Female mammals feed their babies on milk.

REPTILES

Reptile skin is covered with small scales or bigger bony plates. Ocean reptiles include turtles, crocodiles, and snakes, such as the banded sea krait.

INVERTEBRATES

Invertebrates do not have bones inside their bodies. Some, such as crabs, have a hard shell. Others, such as colorful sea slugs, have completely soft bodies.

FAST HUNTERS

Some fierce ocean animals use their speed and strength to catch prey.

These hunters usually have strong teeth for grabbing, slicing, or crushing.

Some hunters, such as saltwater crocodiles, swim gently toward their prey, then make a super-fast dash to snap it up. These muscly reptiles, up to 20 feet (6 m) long, overpower prey easily. Saltwater crocodiles live along the coasts of Australia and southern Asia, in the Indian and Pacific Oceans.

Fast fish have large, smoothly shaped, streamlined bodies, so they can move easily through the water as they chase prey. Sharks are the largest fish of all. The great white shark can swim at up to 35 mph (56 kph). This apex predator also has excellent senses of smell, hearing, and sight to catch prey. It can smell seals up to 2 miles (3 km) away.

A great white shark leaps out of the water to capture a seal, off the coast of South Africa.

FILTER FEEDERS

The biggest, heaviest ocean animal, the blue whale, is not a sharp-toothed hunter.

Like many smaller ocean animals, the largest whales feed by gulping and sucking water.

Up to 100 feet (30 m) long, the blue whale is a filter feeder, along with other baleen whales. These mammals have comb-like structures in their mouths, called baleen plates. They feed by taking gulps of water or swimming with their mouth open. Tiny ocean animals are caught in the combs, filtering them from the water. In one mouthful, a blue whale can swallow 1,100 pounds (500 kg) of krill, small invertebrates found in all the world's oceans.

Some invertebrates, such as sponges, are filter feeders, too. A sponge's body is full of tiny holes and channels, so water can flow through it. Tiny living things and other specks of floating food are trapped inside the sponge. A few birds and fish are also filter feeders, including the flamingo and the world's biggest fish, the whale shark, which grows up to 62 feet (19 m) long.

On a reef in the Caribbean Sea, a stovepipe sponge filters food from the warm water.

Off the coast of Indonesia, a painted frogfish uses its lure to attract prey.

LYING IN WAIT

Another way to catch prey is to sit and wait for it to come by.

Then the predator makes a sudden attack, called an ambush, taking its unlucky prey by surprise.

While waiting for prey, a predator must not be noticed. Some, such as moray eels, hide among coral, rocks, or seagrass. Many ambush predators are colored so they are hard to spot. Frogfish are patterned and shaped so they look like stones or coral.

When prey comes close, moray eels bite fast with their many sharp teeth. These eels also have a second set of teeth in their throat. When an eel has grasped prey in its mouth, the second jaws latch on, moving the food down its throat. Frogfish have a fishing rod-shaped structure between their eyes, with flesh at the end that looks like a little animal. Frogfish wiggle this to attract prey, then suck the prey into their huge mouth.

CLEVER CAMOUFLAGE

Many ocean animals are colored, patterned, or shaped so they blend into their surroundings.

This camouflage is useful for hiding from both predators and prey.

Squid can change their skin color to match their surroundings. Within seconds, they match the pebbles or coral they come across. As firefly squid rise to the ocean surface, they become paler on their underside. This makes them hard to see against the sunlight for predators swimming below.

Seahorses are colored to match their habitat. These little fish can also grow fronds of skin so they look even more like coral or seagrass. Camouflage is important for seahorses as they are poor swimmers due to the bony plates covering their body, preventing them from wriggling. They swim upright by waving their fins. The slowest fish of all is the dwarf seahorse, which moves at 5 feet (1.5 m) per hour.

A pygmy seahorse, shorter than a fingernail, hides among the scarlet coral in the Pacific Ocean.

VICIOUS VENOM

Venom is poison that can kill or stun predators or prey.

Venomous sea animals can inject venom by biting or stinging.

A few animals make venom that stops prey from moving so it can be eaten. Jellyfish hunt by trailing their long tentacles, which have many stinging cells. When touched, these cells shoot venomous arrows into prey. Sea snakes inject their venom through sharp, hollow teeth called fangs.

Venom can also protect animals from attack. Sea slugs eat the stinging cells of sea anemones. The cells do not harm the slugs, but they use them to sting predators. Porcupinefish are too tricky for most predators to swallow, because they are spiky and can swallow water so they blow up like a balloon. Many species of porcupinefish are also venomous, making them disgusting to taste and possibly deadly. Most predators learn to leave them alone.

A Pacific sea nettle jellyfish trails its stinging tentacles, which reach up to 15 feet (4.6 m) long.

In the shallow waters of the western Pacific Ocean, a coconut octopus takes shelter.

HIDE AND SEEK

To avoid being eaten, some ocean animals hide themselves away.

These animals build, borrow, or steal their hideouts.

Octopuses have large brains and have developed clever ways to hide. Many octopuses build dens of rocks, while coconut octopuses find old coconuts or shells to crawl into. Most octopuses can release a cloud of dark ink, which confuses predators and gives the octopus time to escape.

Decorator crabs hide behind other living things or objects. Some cover their shells in pebbles. Others attach non-moving animals, such as coral, sponges, or sea anemones, to their shell. Hermit crabs carry their hiding place with them. These invertebrates are not true crabs, as they do not have a shell. Instead, they climb into the empty shell of a sea snail.

DIVING IN

Many seabirds dive into the ocean to find fish and other prey.

Most grab prey with their beak, but a few use their sharp claws.

Seabirds such as brown pelicans, gannets, and boobies dive into the water from a height. As they fly over the ocean, they watch for prey in the water. Then they tilt their body, fold back their wings – and dive. Falling from heights of up to 100 feet (30 m), they can reach speeds up to 62 mph (100 kph).

Penguins and cormorants dive from the water's surface. Penguins swim through the water with their flipper-like wings. These wings are so well suited to swimming that they cannot be used for flying at all. Cormorants power through the water using their large webbed feet. Webbed feet have skin between the toes, making them like paddles.

A brown pelican plunges into the Atlantic Ocean in search of fish.

Stirring the muddy water with its beak, a roseate spoonbill hunts for prey.

DIPPING IN

Some birds live on the shore, searching for food on beaches and in rockpools.

These shorebirds take advantage of the food-rich zones where ocean and land meet.

Shorebirds have bodies suited to finding food in the shallows or in wet sand and mud. Most shorebirds have long beaks, so they can take prey without putting their heads into water or sand. Differently shaped beaks are useful for different methods of hunting. Common sandpipers poke their sharp beaks into wet sand to find invertebrates. Pink-feathered roseate spoonbills have spoon-shaped beaks that they swing through muddy water to scoop up small fish.

Birds that wade through shallow water are long legged, so their feathers stay dry. A spoonbill's 16-inch (40-cm) long legs make up half its height. The bird's long, widely spread toes stop it from sinking into soft mud.

COMMUNICATION

Ocean animals communicate through sound, touch, and other signals.

They may communicate that they are looking for a mate or they want to hunt together.

Ocean mammals, such as dolphins, usually live in groups. They probably have the most complex communication in the oceans. By touching each other and making clicks and whistles, dolphins show they need help or want to play. Using such signals, dolphins often work together to herd fish, so that they can catch them more easily.

Male fiddler crabs wave their large claws to get a female's attention. Some fish make popping or purring sounds to attract a mate or scare away a rival. Many wrasse and other fish change color when they are ready to mate. The eyelight fish is active at night. To attract a mate, it blinks a light under its eye on and off.

Common dolphins work as a team, herding sardines into an easily captured ball.

Thousands of spider crabs gather for molting in safe and sheltered Port Phillip Bay, Australia.

MIGRATION

At certain times of year, some ocean animals make long journeys across the ocean.

They travel to find safer waters, more food, or to mate.

In winter, thousands of giant spider crabs walk to a bay on the Australian coast in the Indian Ocean. Protected from storms, they can molt safely here, losing their hard shell so they can grow before their new shell hardens. In autumn, spiny lobsters leave the shallow waters of the Atlantic Ocean. They walk to deeper water, where it will be warmer during winter. Each lobster drapes its antennae over the lobster in front so they can stay together.

Some ocean animals travel long distances to find the right place to mate. Sea turtles travel thousands of miles to the beaches where they were born, where they lay hard-shelled eggs in the sand. Many seabirds also fly to the same beach or cliffs on which they hatched.

A male dusky jawfish cradles its eggs in its mouth, in the Atlantic Ocean.

EGGS IN THE WATER

Most fish and many invertebrates lay soft-shelled eggs.

Some look after their eggs until they hatch, while others just swim away.

Most fish and invertebrates do not take care of their eggs. Females release a very large number of eggs. The female ocean sunfish is one of the largest egg producers, releasing 300 million of them. Without a parent to take care of the eggs, many are eaten by predators, but – out of all those millions – some hatch and grow into adults.

A few fish and invertebrates look after their eggs, usually laying just a few hundred. Male jawfish hold the female's eggs in their mouth until they hatch. Female seahorses lay their eggs in a pouch on a male's belly. Many female crabs, lobsters, and shrimps carry their eggs around with them.

On the coast of Namibia, Africa, a mother brown fur seal bonds with her pup.

FAMILY LIFE

For mammals and birds, the stormy oceans are dangerous places to have babies.

These animals usually have just one baby at a time, then take good care of it.

Ocean mammals give birth to live babies. Baby mammals are quite helpless and need to be fed on their mother's milk for days, weeks, or months. Fur seals feed their babies for up to nine months. Many baby mammals stay close to their mother even after they stop needing milk. Some male killer whales stay with their mother as adults.

Most seabirds lay just one hard-shelled egg. Nests are often on cliff ledges, which are difficult for most predators to reach. When chicks are young, parents may take turns to protect the chick and find food. Frigatebirds look after their chick for longer than most birds, spending 14 months keeping them safe. They nest among low branches on remote islands.

GLOSSARY

antennae long, thin feelers found on the heads of some invertebrates

apex predator a hunter so large that it is not usually attacked by other animals

bay a part of the coast where the land curves inward

bird an animal with feathers, wings, and a beak, that lays eggs on land

camouflage body colors and shapes that allow an animal to blend in with its surroundings

cell the smallest working part of a living thing

communication sending and receiving information

coral structures made by tiny animals called coral polyps, which build hard skeletons around their soft bodies

filter to pass water through a structure with holes, removing solids in the liquid

fin a flattened body part used for steering or swimming by fish and some ocean invertebrates and mammals

fish an animal that lives in water, is usually covered in scales, and takes oxygen from the water using gills

food web a series of animals and plants that feed on each other, with bigger predators eating smaller ones

gill a body part that takes oxygen from water

herd to move animals into a group

inject to force a liquid inside the body using a sharp body part or object

invertebrate an animal that does not have a backbone

mammal an animal with hair; female mammals feed their babies milk

mate a partner for making babies

migration moving from one region to another, often at a certain time of year

molt to shed old skin, shell, or feathers

oxygen a gas, found in the air, that animals need to live

plant a living thing that makes its own food from sunlight

predator an animal that eats other animals

prey an animal that is eaten by other animals

reptile an animal with dry, scaly skin

sea anemone an invertebrate animal with stinging tentacles that usually fixes itself to a hard surface

seaweed plant-like algae that grows in the ocean or on the shore

shore the land along the edge of the ocean

stun to make an animal unable to move

venom a poison made by some animals

FURTHER READING

Books

Oceans in Danger! (The Earth at Risk), Alicia Green (Children's Press, 2025)
Ocean Animals (Creature Crafts), Annalees Lim (Wayland, 2017)
Ocean Life (Infomojis), Jon Richards and Ed Simkins (Wayland, 2018)
Wildlife Worlds (series), Tim Harris
(Franklin Watts, 2019)

Websites

Find out more about ocean animals on these websites:

https://oceana.org/marine-life
www.sharktrust.org
www.worldwildlife.org/species/whale

INDEX